IOWA

A PHOTOGRAPHIC CELEBRATION

VOLUME 2

AMERICAN & WORLD GEOGRAPHIC PUBLISHING

GREG CLARK

Above: *Sailor's delight in Marion.*
Right: *A well-earned rest.*

Title page: *The charm of Pella's Dutch culture.* JAMES BLANK

Front cover: *Davenport's landmark Centennial Bridge.* GREG BOLL

Back cover, top: *Autumn silhouettes.*
MARY ELLEN SCHULTZ
Bottom: *Cedar Rapids skyline.*
JAMES BLANK

ISBN 1-56037-029-7

© 1993 American & World Geographic Publishing
P.O. Box 5630, Helena, MT 59604
(406) 443-2842

All editorial work, design and typesetting completed in the U.S.A.
Printed in Korea by Sung In Printing America, Inc., of San Mateo,
California.

Water lily.

Facing page: Fishing at Lake Red Rock.

High-style finance at the old State Exchange Bank Building in Parkersburg.

DAVID CAVAGNARO

Right: *Still life with wild plums, Prunus americana, and food for the soul.*
Below: *How much is that doggy in the window? Probably not for sale at any price. La Porte City.*

Facing page: *It must be past the Fourth of July.*

LARSH K. BRISTOL

The glory of the snow goose.

Facing page: Along the Big Sioux River.

Left: *Running the gamut? Track practice at Dunkerton.*

Below: *A chilly sunrise over the Skunk River at the north end of Ames.*

Facing page: *'Nuff said.*

Old friends at their daily game. Urbana.
Right: *Iowa's oats, corn, and soybeans.*

Facing page: *The golden harvest.*

Above: *Petals in Pella.*
Left: *True grist in northeastern Iowa.*

The spirit of Spirit Lake.

Facing page: *Fort Dodge (1850-53) was one of eight forts the United States established for short periods to control or protect the Indians.*

Fog along the Missouri River.

J.R. WIGGINS

Above: Heritage Farm at Decorah, home of Seed Savers Exchange.
Right: Northeast Iowa, resting over winter.

Facing page: When it grains it pours, in Donahue.

Above: Sparkle of the Iowa State Fair's midway.
Left: Delightful Des Moines.

Typical beauty of Benton County, near Newhall.

Above: *Rock on. Memorial at Clear Lake.*
Right: *From morning to night, there's something to do in this 1910-era former meat-packing plant at Sioux City.*

Above: *An Amish trek to town. Kalona.*
Facing page: *Serenity in the Amana Colonies. Homestead.*

Ottumwa ("rippling waters") has its roots in an 1883 land rush.

Where gamblers can try their luck: casino riverboat at Davenport.

Facing paging, top: *A cottonwood awaiting the sun, near Saylorville Lake.*
Bottom: *The Christmas cheer of Elkader.*

TOM TILL

Sunset adds even more tone to the loess hills of Monona County.

Facing page: *An autumn view at Effigy Mounds National Monument.*

TOM BEAN

Above: *Essence of Iowa, near Atlantic.*
Left: *The Danish Windmill was built in the mid-19th century in Denmark, shipped in pieces to Elkhorn where it was reconstructed.*

Left: I ♥ you all, at mortar(bill)board time. Luther College in Decorah.
Below: Peaceful autumn view of the Mississippi at Lansing.

Facing page: Graceland College Campus. Lamoni.

Below: This veterans' memorial in front of the Denison courthouse was originally established for those who served in the Civil War.

Facing page: Morning approaches Denison.

Right: *It's not just the flowers that add color to Pella's Tulip Time, which is held the second weekend in May.*
Below: *Pella celebrates its heritage with Dutch provincial attire, singing and dancing…*

Facing page: *…and the traditional Tulip Time street scrubbing.*

JACK OLSON PHOTOS BOTH PAGES

A quiet day in downtown Mason City.

Facing page, top: *Chow time at the Living History Farms. Des Moines.*
Bottom: *The Mississippi Queen riverboat navigates her namesake river, as viewed from the Iowa shore.*

Left: *A day the heavens smile on a northeastern farm.*
Below: *Bob Gassman pouring oats into a mixer mill on his farm near Dubuque.*

STEPHEN GASSMAN

West Bend's immense Grotto of the Redemption, started in 1912, contains nine grottoes. Many kinds of minerals as well as fossils and shells were used in the construction.

Above: *This steam-powered stern-wheel museum in Keokuk offers food for the soul of a river-lover.*

Facing page: *Des Moines' State Capitol Building. "Our liberties we prize and our rights we will maintain" is Iowa's motto.*

Below: The Duke's home, in Winterset.

Facing page, top: The three R's, one-room Amish-style. Kalona.
Bottom: In need of starting out with a clean slate. One-room schoolhouse near Denison.

JOHN WAY

Mason City's Meredith Willson Foot Bridge, named in honor of their "Music Man."

JAMES BLANK

The cows in the corn.

Facing page: *May the sun ever shine on the soybean farmer.*

Left: And who would argue?
Bottom left: Oh, to be in Iowa in August.
State Fair, Des Moines.
Below: An autumn picnic at Big Creek
Lake in Polk County.

Right: Autumn leaves me alone in the happiest way.
Below: Enjoying backwaters of the Mississippi River.

Facing page: Yellow River State Forest.

Dubuque, Iowa's oldest city, celebrates the Fourth of July.
Left: *Gamble on your luck aboard Dubuque's Casino Belle.*

LARSH K. BRISTOL

Left: *Commercial fishing near Lansing.*
Below: *There's no such thing as a bad day fishing.*

Facing page: *Did these Guttenberg anglers know they were going ice fishing?*

CLEO FREELANCE

Sailing on Gray's Lake in Des Moines.

Right: Mississippi River north of Bettendorf.

The flavor of Iowa, near Council Bluffs.

CONRAD BLOOMQUIST

TOM BEAN

JACK OLSON

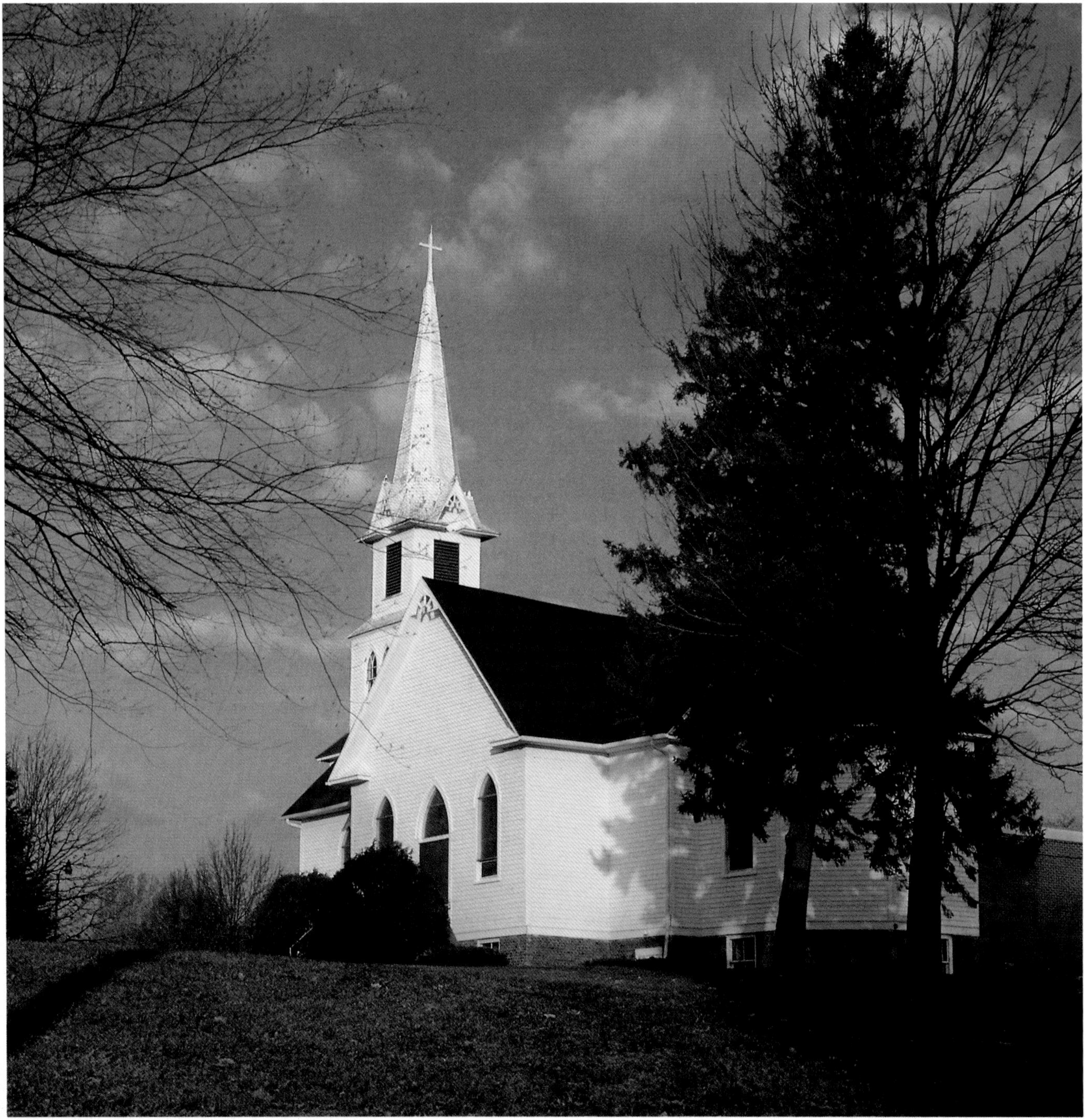

Above: Sunrise, with miles to go before I sleep. RAGBRAI 13, Monticello.
Right: Fourth Street Bridge over Cedar River in Waterloo.

The Living History Farms are hot. Urbandale.

Facing page, top: A prairie crabapple all decked out for spring.
Bottom: The pleasant Main Street of Shellsburg, on Pleasant Creek.

Pages 82 and 83: DeSoto Lake, DeSoto National Wildlife Refuge.

DAVID CAVAGNARO

LARSH K. BRISTOL

Black-eyed Susans in their native prairie habitat, Monona County.

Facing page: *The waterfalls of Boy Scout Camp Klause near Colesburg.*

Light flurries expected.

Facing page: *On the Mississippi hoping for a big strike, near the Lansing Bridge.* LARSH K. BRISTOL

TOM TILL

Above: Asclepias tuberosa, or butterfly weed. Used by early Indians as a remedy, it is also called pleurisy root.
Left: Appreciating the Mississippi River from the bluff in Pikes Peak State Park.

Left: *Is there any other kind?*
Below: *Don't fence me in.*

Facing page: *A view across summer bounty to Marion Lutheran Church, Gunder.*

Left: *Turkey River near El Dorado.* TOM TILL

Below: *The campanile on the Iowa State University campus at Ames.*

Left: *Cedar Rapids skyline along the Cedar River.*

Overleaf: *We're having a bit of weather along the Mississippi.*